Big Sister

Welcoming
Baby Brother
♥ With Love ♥

HELLO
MY NAME IS

And This Is My Book

Mom and Dad said something new,
A little brother is coming, that's true!

I can't wait for that day to come,
To hold my little brother and welcome him home!

We went shopping for baby things to get,
a crib, some toys, and a car seat that fit.

It's bedtime, and I am excited about my baby brother. Wondering what he'll look like and what we'll do together!

I jumped out of bed, feeling so alive.
Today is the day the baby will arrive!

My heart beats fast, and my eyes wide.
My baby brother is right here, by my side!

A baby's skin is soft and new,
So gentle care is what I have to do!

Finally, I got to hold my little brother,
With a heart filled with love like no other.

If little brother cries, he's trying to say, "I need something" in his own baby way.

He might be hungry or need a clean diaper.
Or a hug from his beautiful sister.

I can help with feeding and changing too.
Being a big sister, there's so much to do!

My baby brother needs to stay warm.
We should wrap him up in a cozy blanket to keep him from harm.

My brother loves to explore and taste everything he sees,
So I must ensure he doesn't eat what could make him sick.

And when it's time for our baby to start eating solid food,
I will Make sure to only give him what's healthy and good.

We play peek-a-boo and sing a funny song.
Together we laugh all day long!

Before we go to sleep, we read a book,
My baby brother comes close, and I give him a look!

Sometimes little brother can be quite a bother,
But I will be patient, for I am the older.

My baby brother grows every day,
And we celebrate each milestone along the way!

First smile, first tooth, first crawl, and the first step too,
All are special and unique moments for our family to view!

Being a big sibling is an important role,
loving with all my heart and soul.

Each day we learn something new, my brother and I, as we grow!

Soon we will be older, and our future is bright.
With you by my side, everything feels right!

Sharing is caring; that's what we know.
Every day we watch our love grow!

Even when we will have our own separate lives,
Our love for each other never fades or dies.

Made in the USA
Las Vegas, NV
15 October 2024